Odalisque

MARK SALERNO is the author of *Hate* (96 Tears Press), *Method* (The Figures) and *So One Could Have* (Red Hen Press). *Method* was a Finalist in the National Poetry Series. From 1993 to 1999, he edited *Arshile: A Magazine of the Arts*. His work has appeared in numerous magazines, including *Chicago Review*, *Denver Quarterly*, *Exquisite Corpse*, *First Intensity* and *Talisman*. He is the recipient of a Fund for Poetry award.

Also by Mark Salerno

So One Could Have (2004)
Method (2002)
Hate (1995)

Odalisque

Mark Salerno

CAMBRIDGE

PUBLISHED BY SALT PUBLISHING
PO Box 937, Great Wilbraham, Cambridge CB21 5JX United Kingdom

All rights reserved

© Mark Salerno, 2007

The right of Mark Salerno to be identified as the
author of this work has been asserted by him in accordance
with Section 77 of the Copyright, Designs and Patents Act 1988.

This book is in copyright. Subject to statutory exception
and to provisions of relevant collective licensing agreements,
no reproduction of any part may take place without the written
permission of Salt Publishing.

First published 2007

Printed and bound in the United Kingdom by Lightning Source

Typeset in Swift 9.5 / 13

*This book is sold subject to the conditions that it shall not,
by way of trade or otherwise, be lent, re-sold, hired out,
or otherwise circulated without the publisher's prior consent
in any form of binding or cover other than that in which
it is published and without a similar condition including this
condition being imposed on the subsequent purchaser.*

ISBN 978 1 84471 329 5 paperback

Salt Publishing Ltd gratefully acknowledges
the financial assistance of Arts Council England

1 3 5 7 9 8 6 4 2

Once Again
For
Erna

Contents

Argument	5
Sense	6
Summertime	7
Vernacular	8
At Large	9
Orange Crush	10
Now This	11
Iota	12
The Orange Dress	13
Skirt Consideration	14
To My Far	15
So Do I	16
In An Age	17
Around	18
Offered	19
Collection	20
Gaze	21
Day For Night	22
Depot	23
It Was Not	24
Wah-Wah	25
A Retrospective	26
Still	27
Soliloquize	28
Before She Could	29
Simultaneous	30
Helping Uncle	31

Tethered	32
Solipsism	33
Capping	34
Estimate	35
What I Was	36
Wagons West	37
Fascination	38
No Matter What	39
The Ideal and the Other	40
The Big How-To	41
Finale	42
Heart	43
Eyes Up	44
Generous	45
Statement	46
After All	47
Extended Viewing	48
Some People	49
Pennant	50
Interview	51
In Hours	52
Accessory	53
Lights Out	54
Lie to Me	55
Trouble No More	56

Acknowledgments

Grateful acknowledgment is made to the following magazines, where some of these works previously appeared: *Denver Quarterly*, *First Intensity*, *Pool*, and *Shiny*.

"Extended Viewing," "Some People," "Pennant," "Interview," "In Hours," "Accessory," "Lights Out," "Lie to Me," and "Trouble No More" first appeared in *Lights Out*, published by Beard of Bees Press (http://www.beardofbees.com).

The author offers a much-belated thanks to Jill Stengel and a+bend press for publishing *For Revery*. This acknowledgment was mistakenly omitted from the author's *So One Could Have*.

Grateful acknowledgment is made to Karen Koch, Ron Padgett and The Kenneth Koch Literary Estate for permission to reprint lines from "The Circus" in *The Collected Poems of Kenneth Koch* (New York: Alfred A. Knopf, 2005).

The author thanks William Goldman for permission to reprint lines from *Butch Cassidy and the Sundance Kid* in *Adventures in the Screen Trade* (New York: Warner Books, 1983).

Odalisque

*It is beautiful at any time but the paradox is leaving it
In order to feel it when you've come back . . .*
— Kenneth Koch

*Butch: Would you make that jump if you didn't have to?
Sundance: I have to and I'm not gonna.*
— William Goldman

Argument

To be without believing or fade to the sidelines

as if stranded between cue lines and ordered fragments

a someone until the sex plot wears itself down

or move through another telltale sign of night

my morality she said or lack thereof has gotten me

this far on a set of mile-high heels tits

out to here and an attitude to match

we call it comedy we call it "trade show chic"

because the yellow doesn't begin to describe

the plunge of white or the light conflict when

his moral is easily defeated by his desire

a scrivener within earshot and an odalisque

they came for the show for the little

gasp of red before it all disappears.

Sense

A summed up light certain inches below the fold
and a despised scrivener washed out of the program
I got lost in my address to persons within earshot
as just about everyone on the squad always knew
so you fall back on your training and work the system
the summer after Biggie got shot I gave up my process
because it faded me a little toward the sidelines
along with countless other beauty school graduates
strolling aimlessly past Frederick's of Hollywood
all because a completely new set of logics was lacking
or a small plastic part that is essentially made of green
like the number thirty only when Rick says Paul table thirty
because the geography may be a little difficult to arrange
scattered as we are across a field of green and daylight.

Summertime

In the next decade of his life he becomes as a lost man
on the six feet of concrete outside of Max Factor
a blue of his own devising a static history
paced for a few blocks by the P.D. in a Crown Vic
out here we're paying mostly for the sunlight
just to be driven mad by the sheer joy of it
while she went on being a suntanned odalisque
of a more suntanned and variegated value system
where repeated words became a kind of gaudy patter
to pull against her tether for reassurance or clock out
granted headlong and farfetched granted betrayal
just to make it through the u-shape of life in time
it's how we came to be portioned out in tv light and shtick
a coin toss of the personal faded toward the sidelines.

Vernacular

She repeated the word free and to leave her alone

because they arrived without the alphabet like poor immigrants

to prove a lead pipe logic among shored up fragments

or buy pieces of afternoon light and flunk out

insofar as feeling and being were everywhere apparent

due in part to muffled threnody beyond the primary system

a strange attractor and a backdoor spruce finality

leaning against the stucco at Mayfair Market or

sitting on the backseat with a cold Orange Crush

and *Tiger Beat* because her mind thinks she exists

in tv light to learn simple vocabulary and speaking slowly

notwithstanding h.p. demands d-cup solutions and shtick

like in a road picture a pile-on of widely held beliefs

that fell prey over and over to the double cross of seduction.

At Large

In the rundown big town for who got where

a pile-on of wan beings and summed up light

or pieces of paper with As and Xs and blanks

all are modes of address deep within the eye

I was M. late of the bomb squad and without papers

cut loose among the boots beside The Wiltern LG

for disobeying orders bra logic and dilatory wanderings

as noted in a few good lines below the fold

while she retained the authority of an out of work odalisque

behind a wizardy curtain of seeming and being

what's left is shored fragments and disparate junctures

or thinking seeing and feeling all at the same time

like two-drink minimum poor immigrants under the quota system

of gaudy patter and shtick of betrayal and the regime.

Orange Crush

In simple vocabulary to understand the sex plot dilemma
because they washed up like two-drink minimum poor immigrants
without the alphabet and within earshot of the gold rush
she repeated the word free in the ruse of bra logic
amid gaudy patter farfetched ambition and the transformative other
as if someone just wrote the word odalisque on her ass
despite being wrong and stalling for time backstage at the Pantages
whore talk and beauty school ethics to castigate the real
as summed up in banner headlines from *The Hollywood Reporter*
she got burned in the afterglow the double cross of tv light
notwithstanding a shrewd handling of seeming and being
when the wild card of analysis meets the regime of biology
speaking slowly or mouthing off a.k.a. reason and desire
or drown in this lagoon of flop sweat and untested abstractions.

Now This

The shorter second half and too much articulation
certain amounts of daylight in colored Dixie cups
you and your bomb squad ethics she said I'm tired of
interrogatives tunnel vision cooped up or simply waiting
for a God damned Orange Crush and to be near her
couple-y she said another burning coal down all my life
never heard of Buck-Buck never heard of Acey-Five
because of all the parts left out overnight in TJ
only mention the word moon and you're finished
dream time and clinic noise where M. equals the hero
in fact he is a dream man a blind preoccupation
to enjoy movie star prerogatives from the waist up
or be seen pointing his finger like a teacher
up and down the Strip between Gazzarri's and the Whisky.

Iota

Like muffled foil in a kind of spruce finality

or the logical resting place of hedged bets

I make you no I mar you in the strange attraction

she repeated the word free because she told

her soul to leave her alone like on KTLA

take a minute to memorize some Shakespeare

to distract the mind from its catastrophes

in the next decade of his life he becomes

as a lost man isn't that sticking my neck out

to where all the note said was Ingres was here

an apology not an apostrophe where M. is the

hero who dies over and over again in B movie

oblivion it's a job to stay the heavy train

profligate light green over the hills happy or not.

The Orange Dress

Choosing sides or the bank shot and shtick
accord she said and these are my feelings
air beauty breaklight gesturing at the lunch
he was pompously and so humiliated in fact
he was a dream man and used it like a Polish
blueprint to learn how to do the math
listen to me looking listen to me
racing his baggy ass up the stairs
she was practically naked they fucked she was
burnt umber to pedants and lettered fools
just to make it through the u-shape of life
a no-talent peroxide blonde in go-go boots
which she always regarded as minor adjustments
provisional camping out until finally the money
I am telling you this she said and look up.

Skirt Consideration

Integers of breaklight to check the moon

a complicated remapping that spreads over everything

the keep of you she said and are my things

muffled under the money like Shakespeare

first B. shot dead in L.A. and now my process

in the next decade he becomes as a repeated word

to go headlong into that transit to lose your head

for pictures of people for ways to remember

the lost flint in her which meant deeper trouble

choosing sides in the dust up and staying alive

a slash-and-burn Platonism except the sound

just to make it through the u-shape of life

where nothing is less important than words or

a midnight train to palookaville but not yet.

To My Far

To be sure of my tether that I am not alone
the one who knows versus the one who learns
I won't play the patsy for you or anyone
yellow that lights out the green faked light
the failure of talk the talking cure wan beings
"from rag to rich" the same one-stop dream
immigrants in love my new watch my new vest
and a hell of a good country for a backdoor man
until the odalisque and the threnody and the flop sweat
or one day a blonde in a little red ragtop
his diffident salvage job to gather the wind
schmaltzy and foreign sounding and the timing off
like working for the bomb squad over and over
to play the patsy for the odalisque to be sure.

So Do I

Who got lost what got saved give account

as if it mattered it's ours to bother with

a d-cup solution to the think-think track

where nothing is more worthless than words

for wan beings to scruple and clock out

to go to school on the field of battle

or draw a line around seeming and being

part of it was right the Zankou Chicken part

in ten years hair dye and a new set of teeth

a Polish blueprint for the u-shape of life

when we stop doing this it will all be over

this look at me solution to the foreign sounding

part of it was true the made-up part

it means we go back to square one which equals us

an idea a person a dog a cat a something.

In An Age

Perception acknowledgment or ways to tinker
a history of incarnadine days of thunder
alive beside the brickout what else was there
for mojo light spangling the sex plot dilemma
specifically all the things her voice contained
and a lawn of green racing its baggy ass up the hill
the memory world of the artist is relevant again
it is the upside down cake of all our reveries
they maintain their presence as abstract gestures
what we missed in the day-long tirade to address each other
I am "t" she said like a thousand handfuls of air
in streets in apartments in offices in cities
how far off I sat and wondered while we looked for
a brilliant something tall enough to scrape the stars.

Around

Scare tactics running gags and out in the open

to find treasure using a treasure map

or losing all have I now lost my mirth

for a few faint images of life down at McDonald's

no my lord that was a phantom a phantom of clouds

to reward the eye and or relieve the ear

neon before the fall the car wash and candy store

I was M. I was the hero like non-blink solution

all night trying the handles on parked cars

it's how we came to be measured our portion

of breaklight cue lines and a handful of ludes

when sounding wrong becomes one way of being right

not forgetting wan beings bra logic and shtick

in the exact fitment of everything that has become of us.

Offered

Clinics hedged bets and what's been bruited about
a bunch of below compass wan beings cashiered
and living under a hard star it's air beauty
she repeated the word free an odalisque at
the automat and in effect he was a dream man
just to find out if two people if [if if]
what is saved is threnody breaklight and shtick
a beauty school pageant in which Lazy Susan
meets the dumb waiter they share an Orange Crush
still the sense is cooped up and within earshot
of what could have been a nice salvage job
that closes a door on the noise of the heart
but every map tells the same diffident story
you are here just when here could be anywhere.

Collection

Waiting in shirt sleeves beside the FedEx truck

or with the bomb squad until your number's up

what's down is louts and Platonic shadows

taking lumps and following a Polish blueprint

someone's patsy in the emotional rain

the zigzag of desire headlong in the crush

like life itself when she said certain words

to cast more light into this Pep Boys flop sweat

I was M. on suspension for mouthing off

not to mention dilatory wanderings and simultaneous aspects

sticking my neck out for a no-talent peroxide blonde so be it

or just to get through the u-shape of life as is

granted headlong granted idolatry and farfetched ambition

to give credence and scruple or leave her alone.

Gaze

Rising to the surface and what it had to do with

because my subject is directional it includes

desire and attendant clamor beating on someone's door

all day and half the night beside the Cahuenga newsstand

for a pair of go-go boots and what amounts to bra logic

she was she she brought the air back to everyone's lungs

no matter possession anger and the thwarted demands

just when the central character sneaks out for a smoke

to regard the surface to listen and ask questions

like on *Columbo* it's our only way of knowing

I was M. until I dropped off the emotional radar

there's an upside to the downside it's called shadowland

that sails out of the grasp of poor preoccupation

camouflage palette idolatry and a whole week of rain.

Day For Night

Just when my pencil strays from realism and
my more narrow sense of being what arrives
is breaklight h.p. demands and a blown-fuse
idealism to be filled in by the late-comers
I was M. now headlong into the d-cup solution
desire for possession art for money time for time
it's a conflict without resolution without
much of a chance and a stinker at the box office
something like a veil was lifted at Bally Total Fitness
the regime of the personal floated away in
its little dinghy amid cartoon ticker tape
in air the color of light about a dime's worth
the double cross your heart of seduction again
a trick photography plot knocked off its folding chair.

Depot

Detuned and ripe for cozening or just verging
on agreement slack like a hairdresser's dummy
it's a love story ape a potluck sex plot
as if seeing thinking and feeling all at once
while parked for an hour in front of Little Toni's Pizza
I was thinking of those poor marielitos who first
came to Gatsby's parties the summer after Biggie
and my process and how it faded me a little
the idolatry of reason will fuck you up
ciphering a memory of the way she said couple-y or
leaning on another bromide in order to relearn the scissor kick
thanks to a shoe box full of grainy before the war photographs
for an odalisque parts I got wrong or didn't understand
when it mattered words to look up and then the hatcheck.

It Was Not

Vain belief and or the position of modern illusionism

marking time with the bomb squad until your number's up

another despised scrivener who can't get off the contents page

I was M. and for a while I was my double in the Tuff Shed

it had to do with hacking up the disquiet and common enough

to feel tailored and bespoke to have a "right light" moment

instead of a lifetime in the back offices of Preview House

she was correct to be the air in someone's lungs

but how far out of Kingstown did you expect to get

with just pantyhose and a cinder block way of thinking

buying time and making payments into the double cross

or last chances that gutter balled over negative space

it might as well have snowed could have snowed did snow

if I kissed your footsteps as I have scrupled to aver.

Wah-Wah

Whatever much has been bruited about a sugary turn
more wan beings look at them clinging to a leaf
or useless ornament a country stamped out of tin
until some scrivener some Shakespeare on the breakfast plan
got cashiered bounced really and in a tv light
I'm prepared to match regrets with any of you soldiers
in palettes that made Staten Island look like Provence
I was M. late of the bomb squad and everyone's patsy
shaky handwriting and a damn good cry beside the Victrola
like Ingres shitfaced again and half out of his pants
what's left is muted a scaled-down sense and longing
otherwise this new geometry is practically folly proof
kicking the leaves as we go and breathing in
because one is always looking for new ways to be foiled.

A Retrospective

Lacked a live replacement or Live Nude Girls

not estimating a nickel bag of what's probative or in the air

the u-shape of life while working from a Polish blueprint

given we were not quite equals in the ruse of bra logic

what's reflected is blue and the green more simply

breaks off the talking cure into h.p. demands and cue lines

or shouting oneself hoarse down at Irv's Burgers

to pull back the wizardy curtain on muffled longing

immigrant pin-ups and discount store solutions

like Biggie in the drive-by as the desert night collapsed

I had thought this no man's land would be smaller

and so got stony stuttering out the prelude

more spit-take shtick to save a fairy tale with you

and no picnic given the beeline of blind preoccupation.

Still

Tooling along these mountain roads in my garbage truck
to dilate upon landscape but with all the trees erased
adequate to the task but lacking brick and mortar charm
some cutie girl his one great subject hard to perceive
I'm speaking to your hole Thisbe can you hear me now
flesh was the reason oil paint was invented and just to
stay alive a little longer with or without the alphabet
I was M. in the pile-on of a few good lines below the fold
man bites odalisque sundry particulars a roadhouse a roadhouse
while the tin whistle economy at work in the leaves
too quiet for a young country and the reason Thoreau
gave up the memory world of the artist is relevant again
wherein a new-guy class war going on down at Tom's Number 5
poverty that would make you laugh and of course it rained.

Soliloquize

Interrupted but to be wholly at ease I scrupled

reason enough in consequence to leave out the I

a limned conflict for plot it has to be there or

who will pay attention to these disparate junctures

she was her own kind of bright a blue plate special

in the general rout of discounted afternoon light

excepting of course a gallon of Henry's left on the roof

poverty that would make you laugh and my desire

to draw back the wizardy curtain on go-go boots the d-cup

solution and hours of bra logic little slut that I was

amounted to the moral equivalent of the "Shoop Shoop Song"

if only we could fasten the wind or box up clouds

dwindling down to an idea too big for its britches and so

opposition and derision and cashiered from the bomb squad.

Before She Could

We *coincided* in light of what I later learned
pushing aside my supposed wrong ideas *to fuck*
in position and nervous as I was *I knew* right away
all of the problems would be beautifully loosened but
he came ready with *sentences* to resist what he'd started
I had to settle him down even though he knew my tricks
with words *he flooded me* so I told him he'd have to *stop*
pointing his finger like a teacher given my small-town
beginnings he took me carefully and fed me and *I knew*
a discourse that dissipates a waking kind of dream
a dream of possession according to him *my biology*
blocking his way with my hips *he couldn't see me*
his analysis was that I should find someone else
beyond the primary system of his or my desires.

Simultaneous

Gathered in or gathered up in position of the modern

in a young country shouting itself hoarse to resist

the regime of the personal and a nosedive into bra logic

I was M. late of the bomb squad and too big for my bridges

the wild card this time and brazen as nails

but how far did you expect to get in French tips and gaudy patter

my guerdon a Polish blueprint for the u-shape of life

headlong as I was in this summed up light and she like

potluck itself coming through the doors of The Broadway Hollywood

later to be thought of as the air from anyone's lungs

all because it suited the terms of the primary system

one day someone says the word odalisque one day

an unimportant scrivener is sentenced under The Pottery Barn Rule

on orders from higher up in the general crackdown of desire.

Helping Uncle

To witness our concerns or just forget the dream

this nattering sense of green in the day-long idolatry

of bra logic and go-go boots little slut that I was

another two-drink minimum poor immigrant shipwrecked

in shadowland without the alphabet or any kind of a clue

to get through the u-shape of life memorizing Shakespeare

or just idling in the faint scenes behind Kaiser Permanente

it's how we came to be wan beings under opposition and derision

marielitos washed up on Gatsby's lawn the summer after Biggie

in L.A. despite blind preoccupation or shoring up my process

and she was a fair piece of work her own kind of trophy

until the breaklight and the inconclusive other and the

fairy tale within earshot as I have scrupled to aver.

Tethered

Ambiguous because coincidental and so drawn awkward

more below compass wan beings battling up a hill

of beans possession and someone else's sex plot dilemma

hedged bets before the talking cure covered under the HMO

I was M. late of the bomb squad and wobbly on my pins

the idea being that if two people despite the ongoing illusionism

to finally pull back the wizardy curtain on the real dream

as seen in fragments due in part to a spangly uncertain light

wherein the cashiered expert because it all blows up in his face

and she becomes as an out of work odalisque

killing time between sessions in the hospital cafeteria

small-town beginnings and a lead pipe logic that didn't get far

below the fold roughed up for sticking her neck out

until the noise and the door and a kind of feeling.

Solipsism

Face to face and eye to eye close enough to hear
in the distance an accent of green a green light contemplated
what had one wanted so to be but here in company
notwithstanding a little lost and let's face it dwindled down
a two-people plot marred by derision and opposition
until one day he becomes headlong he becomes as a lost man
late of the bomb squad and killing time in Bob's Big Boy
while she survived as her own kind of recuperating subject
on mile-high heels tits out to here and an attitude to match
another odalisque that got ground up in the afterglow
of h.p. demands cue lines and a handful of ludes
pie-eyed with immigrant logic just to be in the picture
or hack one's way through the u-shape of life as is
to shore up a few fragments to sum up I was M.

Capping

Stars on pieces of paper and a decade of walking away
arising out of the inconclusive headlong sans alphabet
practically pie-eyed with grief because she said couple-y
transforming the figurative into the double cross of seduction
as noted under The Pottery Barn Rule and anterior quota system
Biggie set up in L.A. just when I gave up my process
forgoing the lead pipe logic and wafts of Skin Bracer
an odalisque in matching bra and panties a girl on the job
those marielitos saw as we did something extraordinary in G.
the default position of a young country longing to be modern
despite a little trouble with that lust for killing thing
I was M. late of the bomb squad and washed out of the program
which is what you get for mouthing off in the general crackdown
of propositions like spy vs. spy love vs. love and live vs. die.

Estimate

To keep oneself free and the regime of the personal
in shored up distinctions between seeming and being
but the two people plot fades towards the sidelines
for another no-talent peroxide blonde in go-go boots
relegated to the customer service desk at Pic 'N' Save
while he was a dream man ill-equipped and without the alphabet
to save a fairy tale of scenes drenched in penny arcade light
a within earshot ciphering of the way she said couple-y
or what might be summed up in the back pages of *Tiger Beat*
rewritten as immigrants longing for a crack at the big time
beyond clinics beauty school day jobs and threnody
to save this much but my undoing was blind preoccupation
leaning on the john door in the 5 SPOT as proof
in the general crackdown of true life in the far west.

What I Was

Consequent upon disparities of seeming versus being
out on the coast and waiting for a right light moment
wherein the zigzag of desire meets the u-shape of life
she repeated the word free because she told her soul
to leave her alone another shipwrecked odalisque adrift
in the two people plot and he was a dream man washed up
on the sidelines of blind preoccupation and handfuls of air
something like a veil was lifted at Bally Total Fitness
I was M. late of the bomb squad and hell-bent for leather
to give credence to the world of appearances or buck up
lists of flowers pet names names of children and drug lore
go-go boots bra logic and the d-cup solution chasing down
the sex plot dilemma and throwing money little slut that I was
to fasten on the regime of green light and the primary system.

Wagons West

Stranded on a paint-chipped shoreline like wan beings
what had one thought in sentences and stuttered words
noting brackets of green light surrounding the photo booth
one's cashiered other self picks over the below compass damage
twenty years ago potluck derision and folding chair ethics
I was M. another two-drink minimum poor immigrant
adrift among hedged bets and brazen as nails
until one day she decided to draw a line around herself
to put modern illusionism aside for a lungful of air
or what might be found in far arcades at the Burbank IKEA
because she knew my tricks and came ready to clock out
of the love versus money detective novel the story story
like G. said she was tired of waiting and reasonable enough
given the headlong and the u-shape as I have scrupled to aver.

Fascination

Day-long a hard saying and finally shored up

loose arrangements because of the double impact

of identity a preposterous farrago animated with life

to save a fairy tale of a dream man and an odalisque

or gutter ball across negative space into the headlong

I was M. a cashiered expert and kicked off the squad

weighing the relative merits behind Jumbo's Clown Room

of a no-talent peroxide blonde in go-go boots or fade

to the sidelines with the other undocumented workers

while she went on being her own transgressed argument

a sex plot know it all in sheer slip and mules to start

the potluck all over again Ph.D. night at the bingo parlor

and the end of the line summed up by another despised scrivener

a more potent saying within earshot or just forget the dream.

No Matter What

The inconsistent other and a usual fall from grace

because repetitive of unfinished logics and making tracks

caught in the double cross despite sticking my neck out

I was M. before I fell below compass in the primary system

and gave up my process the summer after Biggie got shot

what's left is threnody muffled under the money like Shakespeare

to become headlong in the d-cup solution whore talk and go-go boots

after some hard hours at the juice bar of Bally Total Fitness

while her delight was to pull against her tether and be in position

as a gloss on tv light and the regime of the personal

transforming the way she said couple-y into the raiment of my heart

another credence between seeming and being the world of appearances

or scare tactics running gags flop sweat and French tips

with or without the alphabet and out in the open at last.

The Ideal and the Other

Day-long in the breaklight to arrive at her finality

as if gun-shy in regard to the short fuse of h.p. demands

it's a risky business and absent of viable alternatives

to conflate seeming and being like a costumed odalisque

bra cups and boobie traps littering the sex plot dilemma

if only two people over and over until the mind surrenders

and the obvious subject of all my reveries to date I was M.

roughed up in the afterglow of flop sweat shtick and running gags

sidelined along with all the other beauty school graduates

or working the late shift behind the bar at Hamburger Hamlet

just to be within earshot of the way she said couple-y

notwithstanding muffled under authority and given the boot

when the idolatry of reason finds its logical resting

place in opposition and derision.

The Big How-To

Prone to a strange attraction in the general crackdown
and the day my document if only to repeat or shore up
if only to make it through the u-shape of life in time
granted headlong granted whore talk and the d-cup solution
or waiting it out on the back seat with a pop and a *Tiger Beat*
I was M. busted in the ranks and willing to keep it simple
while she went on to become an ex-odalisque and inconclusive
chastened by the memory of immigrant logic and tunnel vision
another salvage job out of earshot of the muffled longing
what's left is threnody breaklight and a cooped up sense
to pull back the wizardy curtain on below compass wan beings
the double cross of seduction or just forget the primary system
insofar as we are always betrayed by the world of appearances
and plummet between seeming and being as I have scrupled to aver.

Finale

To be without believing or just forget the dream

as when a former odalisque too late to get lucky

settles on a set table in a dingy outlying suburb

she told her soul to leave her alone and it did so

chastened by the memory of true life in the far west

and a little roughed up in consequence of feeling

when giving up becomes one way of staying alive

I was M. dilatory in my wanderings and a lost man

hustled by a cutie girl and drenched in flop sweat

for my anxiety to know the really real or breathe air

between seeming and being of the way she said couple-y

along with all the other beauty school graduates

cooped up and portioned out running gags and shtick

to save a fairy tale as I have scrupled to aver.

Heart

To present several aspects simultaneously or mouthing off

as a way of knowing the really real in the breaklight in shadowland

or lose oneself headlong in d-cup solutions sans apostrophe

considering a bunch of cashiered two-drink minimum poor immigrants

a hard saying given foreign sounding and cooped up below the fold

just to make it through the u-shape of life under the primary system

the summer after Biggie got shot sordid greed and cheap vainglory

and an odalisque who once resembled a gangster's moll

washed up and dilatory among the rush at Roscoe's Chicken and Waffles

the reason being as everyone on the squad always knew

sooner or later something blows up in your face

short fuses boobie traps gaudy patter and a farfetched inkling

cut down to size by the double cross of seduction

insofar as one is tripped up between seeming and being.

Eyes Up

Day-long in the breaklight but the feeling is cooped up

an aftermath wherein nothing is settled nothing refrained

but scare tactics bra logic boobie traps and gaudy patter

below compass you had to have the front page pulled tight

it's the position of derision without which I was headlong

another despised huckleberry stranded at Bullocks Wilshire

when each hesitating moment amounted to a close call

like two-drink minimum poor immigrants awash in Skin Bracer

if only two people alone could make it to the end of the line

the summer after Biggie got shot I gave up my process

and became as a lost man within earshot of the threnody

to give credence to the world of appearances or crap out

cashiered and roughed up a former expert cut down to size

between seeming and being to save a fairy tale I was M.

Generous

Akin to feelings of suspension or drop kicked for naught

just to make it to the candy counter before the front crawl

between being and believing and find oneself without the dream

shuffled in among the weekday crowd in front of Grauman's Chinese

more immigrants under a burden of Skin Bracer and plural identities

while she became a former odalisque now retired to the suburbs

with new recipes of how to stay beyond the reach of the threnody

the two-people plot that got her a little trouble in town

for being expository air when what she wanted was couple-y

a road picture wherein all of the problems are beautifully loosened

in several simultaneous aspects flop sweat and running gags

to save a fairy tale for portion to have a right light moment

tethered as we are to one blind preoccupation or another

and bruited about in h.p. demands cue lines and a handful of ludes.

Statement

Out of luck and cut down to size in the afterglow
to give credence just when I became headlong
and adrift in d-cup solutions little slut that I was
to make it through idolatry with the front page pulled tight
wan beings flunky cops beauty school stars and seduction
transforming tv light into ways to forget the dream
Biggie set up at Petersen's and a defunct primary system
I was M. late of the bomb squad and no longer significant
within the circuit of blind preoccupation at Musso and Frank
for a no-talent peroxide blonde in go-go boots a moll
insofar as the inconclusive other buys a little time
the first betrayal is always the betrayal of reason
when feeling amounts to a salvage job and immigrant finality
wishing that daylight or any light would simply disappear.

After All

To be without believing and finally give up the dream
or shouting oneself hoarse down front at the Troubadour
a bunch of below compass wan beings their cases set
cashiered and given the boot under the regime of right reason
the reward of h.p. demands cue lines and a handful of ludes
it's the logical resting place of opposition and derision
I remembered those poor marielitos washed up on Gatsby's lawn
before anyone's analysis had happened to us yet
immigrants one way or another we are all between engagements
to pull back the wizardy curtain on running gags and shtick
after the first betrayal you get canned and lose everything
for mouthing off like in a road picture to shore up fragments
insofar as gaudy patter becomes its own meaningful boobie trap
the wild card of seduction tv light and the transforming figurative.

Extended Viewing

Static or farfetched but nonetheless to give credence

of a few faint images or parts where it got dicey

Biggie set up at Petersen's and then the summer

my elm won't leave me alone it is memory it is nothing

I was M. late of the Miracle Mile washed up and cut down

under authority of The Pottery Barn Rule no longer relevant

while she became a former odalisque retired to the suburbs

amid theatrical mementos old headshots and publicity stills

abiding in the space that comes after everything happens

insofar as seeming and being is always the first betrayal

a proving ground for wan beings of opposition and derision

they arrived like two-drink minimum poor immigrants

pie-eyed with grief or headlong in various d-cup solutions

caught up in the action the general crackdown of desire.

Some People

Staying alive and making it through the u-shape of life

notwithstanding being hacked up in the day-long idolatry

to relearn credence blind preoccupation and sticking your neck out

in lieu of simple vocabulary and right light moments

the first betrayal is the betrayal of seduction

her analysis was to give up and go home a retired odalisque

therefore the movie ends on a railway platform at Union Station

surrounded by two-drink minimum poor immigrants and breaklight

they came to the new world to get laid

drink wine and laugh themselves to death

in clinics in night schools in walk-ups in day jobs

while I was M. sacked from the bomb squad and no longer relevant

insofar as headlong for a no-talent peroxide blonde in go-go boots

the inconclusive other but dicey as I have scrupled to aver.

Pennant

She repeated the word free she repeated the word couple-y

to get laid they came here and with all of the problems

notwithstanding seduction running gags and a handful of ludes

to stay the heavy train or keep August off the dumb waiter

foiling the plot just when modern illusionism summed up

a crackdown on orders from the D.A. cashiered under authority

to press for the regime of the personal little slut that I was

in the next decade he gave up his process and became as a lost man

insofar as the first betrayal is boobie trapped with bra logic

pretty soon it will all be in English except in Los Angeles

in tv light or below compass or flunking out of beauty school

to pull back the wizardy curtain on being and believing

the people people heaved up under trellises of air or

beautifully loosened to leave her soul alone I was M.

Interview

It ends in opposition and derision in order to be visible
for this she drew a line around herself her I her me
and retired out of earshot of some various muffled threnody
to put aside a strange attraction or just forget the dream
a former wan being who got a little roughed up in the afterglow
pulling against her tether to make it through the u-shape of life
and finally close a door on pedants and lettered fools
soon it will all be in English except the noise of the heart
or shouting oneself hoarse after that thing at Staples Center
if only it relieves the ear and or rewards the eye if only [if if]
in this burden of being a song and dance man gaudy patter and shtick
the moral equivalent of bra logic given the wild card of seduction
and in any case backed into or out of the regime of the personal
with both of us drawing lines around what she said and who she was.

In Hours

It ends in bra logic and failed transitive devices

just to advance from one headlong desire to another

notwithstanding our cooped up notions of a primary system

or tunnel vision flop sweat and shtick to save a fairy tale

it's how we got canned under the regime of reason

the summer after Biggie got shot I gave up my process

because it faded me a little toward the sidelines

I was M. no longer significant in the general crackdown

for a no-talent peroxide blonde in go-go boots

she was brazen as nails to give credence to the world

insofar as cue lines amounted to the dream itself

sticking my damn neck out for whore talk at Steve Boardner's

and shoring up fragments like all the other poor immigrants

or mouthing off to authority for an odalisque I was M. I was M.

Accessory

More wan beings in panoramas of their own imaginings
or mixing in with the breakfast crowd at Denny's on Sunset
they came to the new world to get laid and freak out
in right light moments sordid greed and cheap vainglory
it was a way to be significant without recourse to the alphabet
when the double cross of seduction presented several aspects
a pile-on of widely held beliefs and plural identities
hence one grateful tether to rein her in and connect her
to the world of being under authority and castigation
along with all the other beauty school graduates roughed up
repeating the word free and killing time on the back seat
pretty soon it will all be in English or muffled under the money
the summer after I gave up my process to save a fairy tale
another summed up light in the general crackdown of desire.

Lights Out

A little roughed up and so mouthing off under authority
stranded between seeming and being in fact thrown off the squad
for a no-talent peroxide blonde in go-go boots as occurs
in the next decade of his life he becomes no longer significant
wondering what's left of our lungs and the brightly colored air
she repeated the word free and told her soul to shut up
on faint scenes of life and numerous assorted fragments
while my part was cut down to a few lines at the end
from a synopsis that could have been found in the back pages of *Tiger Beat*
Barney's Beanery Duke's The Power House The Side Show El Carmen
flunky cops beauty school graduates despised scriveners and seduction
on mile-high heels tits out to here and a small-town history
insofar as being famous was an end in itself
notwithstanding stupid mistakes and the fall back position of
    blind preoccupation.

Lie to Me

It amounted to a salvage job but there you're on your own
in twilight a few paces behind the big shots at Fred Segal
memory that just has to jackhammer your brain for a while
as you wonder if you could ever be relevant again
suppose I didn't care anymore about her hands or what she said
as though she were just another dumb odalisque on Hollywood Blvd.
new in town and working from a Polish blueprint and mistakes
to be the one who knows versus the one who learns as occurs
when the idolatry of reason got cashiered for fame itself
and the concomitant h.p. demands cue lines and a handful of ludes
it got headlong living below compass to shout oneself hoarse
like two-drink minimum poor immigrants and pie-eyed to be here
until one day it all blows up in your face
I was M. I was the hero this is my story.

Trouble No More

When thinking of his feelings he imagined it as carefree

having relearned risk management on the roof of Hollywood High

because he thought the years of tv light and reason were behind him

he went his own way and took his lumps for it end of story

in the movie the renegade cop resists the system and does good

by transforming the figurative and shoring up useless fragments

he was just seeing himself as unlucky he was playing the sap

if you step over the line once you get smacked you get canned

or sometimes you just find yourself over the line

he thought of himself as below compass and good to go

notwithstanding several aspects simultaneously and a lead pipe logic

immigrants beauty school graduates scriveners and the like

sentenced under The Pottery Barn Rule and mouthing off to authority

long after the point of speaking slowly and simple vocabulary.

Lightning Source UK Ltd.
Milton Keynes UK
UKHW010643250320
360860UK00001B/51